A Real G's Story

ISBN: 978-1-7341346-8-1

LOC Control #: 2020905823

Copyright © Reveena Blair

Publisher, Editor and Back Cover Graphics:

Fiery Beacon Publishing House

Fiery Beacon Consulting and Publishing Group

Front Cover Graphics: Henry James

This work was produced in Greensboro, North Carolina, United States of America.

A Real G's Story

By

Reveena Blair

Table of Contents

THE DEDICATION

The Dedication

This book is dedicated to the three people who have helped to shape my life:

To my parents, Linda Forbes and the late Deacon Curtis Blair:

Thank you for supporting me when no one else would.

To my Spiritual Mother, Apostle Dr. Serena Harris:

Thank you for not giving up on me, even when I wanted to.

Chapter 1

They say the only time that we as Christians should look back over our past is to see how far God has brought us; well I beg to differ. I am thankful for what God has done in my life but as I looked back, I saw every hurt, pain and broken promise that I had not yet healed from. I would be lying if I said that I did not love being in sin. I have lived a life some young women would dream of and some would be afraid of living. Every moment of my life was not peaches and cream, but it was not all bumps and bruises either.

Life is like a journey so to speak - a road trip with endless stops and God is your GPS. Some stops are full of pleasure and fun but the other stops are more like bathroom breaks and flat tires; either way it is up to you to trust the GPS that knows the way or go the way you want to go and figure it out on your own. I want to share some of my life's journey with you. There are parts that made me sad and angry and moments that filled me with joy. Every obstacle I have had to face, all the trials and tribulations I have dealt with and every moment has made me who I am today. Even the mess I found myself in and especially the ones I created myself, worked FOR me. Romans 8:28 says:

"and we know that all things work together for good to them that love God, to them who are called according to His purpose."

Even though I did not understand the call then, everything still worked for my good - the good, bad and the ugly. I am the youngest of three children, the apple of my father's eye and spoil just a little bit. I cannot remember a time I ever needed or wanted something as a child that I did not receive it. My parents worked very hard, so we did not have to live or experience a hard lifestyle. I was never neglected as a child and I had loving parents and siblings. So how did I end up in this kind of life? Why did I make so many bad choices continually? I have done many things that I am not proud of. I am not ashamed anymore, but I am certainly not proud of them. I wish I knew then what I know now. Even through all the darkness God had a plan for my life that I knew nothing about.

I had a pretty normal and good childhood. My family had its pros and cons just like everyone else's. My parents did not always get along, but they always made sure we had everything that we needed and that we were well taken care of. My mom worked like a Jamaican - multiple jobs and long hours. I do not believe there is a field of work that my mom has not tapped into yet. Despite all the hours she worked, she still managed to spend time with us. My dad was a smart and hard-working man. He was also an extremely strict disciplinarian, but when you were on his good side, he was so lovable and kind to everyone. He battled with drugs when I was younger; that does not change the fact that he was a great father and a remarkable man. When I was a little girl all I had to do was make my daddy a hot dog or peanut butter and jelly sandwich and just like that, I was off punishment. (Trust me I stayed on punishment a lot back then.)

My sister is six years older than me and I have always envied her. It seems she could do no wrong in my mother's eyes and I wanted to be just like her. She walked the straight and narrow path. Looking back now, it almost seems funny that I was actually jealous of my sister. She had problems and trials just like I did, but when you are young you do not see that; all I saw was that she got more attention than I did from my mother. Now as I look at her, I am so proud of the wife, mother, sister, aunt and friend she is today. She is kind, lovable, a great listener and certainly a protector. I have learned so much from her over the years and she does not even know It.

My awesome brother and I are only three years apart and he is a character. He is funny and carefree. He has a learning disability, but you cannot tell him that. He is now married with four kids of his own; I think He did a pretty good job. My brother was never raised to think he had a disability; he knows he can be or do anything that he puts his mind to do.

So, let's get to me, shall we? To understand the why, you must know the who. I have always been very smart. My mother used to say I had a gift for gab. I could talk my way in or out of just about anything. I could take someone else's idea and make it a masterpiece. Trouble did not have to find me because I have always seemed to find trouble. Growing up, I was not a bad kid. if you asked my parents, they would probably say something totally different, so I guess I may have been a bit of a handful back then. Needless to say, I stayed in trouble in school and at home a lot, mostly because I had a smart mouth. I had absolutely no problem with my grades. I always made the Honor Roll list. I am a researcher and love to learn new things. I was smart, sometimes too smart for my own good. So how did I get into this life? How did a spoiled brat from Virginia turn into a real gangster, liar, drug user, pimp and a serious whoremonger? I became someone I was not proud of and someone I did not recognize for a long time.

Chapter 2

I remember the day like it was yesterday — the day that changed my life forever. It was my thirteenth birthday and my dad let me have a house party, and after the party I stayed at my best friend's house. We snuck out so she could go see her boyfriend and that was when I saw him - a seventeen-year-old dope boy that every girl had a serious crush on in my neighborhood. Back in my day, all the cool kids hung out in abandoned houses (we called them "the bammas.") Since it was illegal to have an empty house without lights and water on it was the perfect place for teenagers to hang out. I remember the music playing and the smell of weed in the air. My crush walked me past a dozen guys and a few girls to one of the bedrooms in the back of the house. I was a little nervous since I had never gone "all the way" with a guy before. That night I received a crash course of sex 101. As we were making out on the floor, I heard the door open and close. I turned to see three other boys in the room. I remember being pulled, hit then pinned down as I screamed and yelled. Of course, no one came to help, and no one heard the loud screams. After being hit a few more times I just stop fighting. I closed my eyes as the tears dripped down my cheek and focused on the music. I laid still on the floor, in pain as these four young

14

boys took turns on top of me. When they were done with me, one guy stepped on my stomach on his way out; my crush spit on me and they all laughed. I do not remember how long I laid there crying with blood all over my bottom torso. At last I heard a female voice then an unknown man picked me up and took me back to my friend's house.

This was the first time I was raped but certainly not the last. The rape changed me but that is not what truly damaged me. The police were called and so were my parents. My father showed up right after the paramedics. No doubt, in my mind, he was probably high as a kite. I will never forget the way he looked at me at that very moment as if I disgusted him. "What did you do?", my dad asked me while the paramedics started an IV in my arm. Those four words would replay in my mind for years to come.

For years I felt that I was not good enough. I felt as if I had somehow disappointed everyone in my life that meant something to me. I begin to act out severely - drinking, smoking and running away from home at the age of fourteen. My mother tried everything to pull me back on the right track. I was sent to counseling, took medication, and sent to an alternative school; finally, I was placed in a home for troubled teens. It seems the more people tried to help me, the worse I became. I was falling into a hole and it was bigger than anyone could see on the outside. By the time I was fifteen or sixteen I had a few hustles going on. I also realize that I liked girls and they liked me. I was dressing like a female but acting like a boy. I was very rough around the edges. I told myself that a guy could not do nothing for me but hand me some cash. I had no problem fighting a guy or a girl. The wall that I had built up was high and I dared anyone to test me or try to climb it.

I have always been a hustler by nature; I can survive in any environment because I know how to adapt. One of my hustles I ran was getting young girls to steal clothes from the mall so that I could sell them to customers that place orders with me. That is how I met a woman that would teach me how to use my many gifts. She was an exotic dancer and took me to my first party. I watched how the women talked, moved and what they had to do to get paid more. After my first night of watching and seeing how much money they made I wanted in! I learned how to dance and perfected my craft. I learned the game quickly. Young ladies wanted to be like me, and every man wanted me. I was sixteen with a body of a twenty-two-year-old and I used every bit of it.

Every once in a while, I would go to church with a family member; this is where I found my voice. I was always told I could sing but it was different in church. God gave me a gift with no expectations. I did not have to be like anyone else and no one was throwing in my face that someone else was better than me. I was free to be me. The church did not care who I was on the streets or my faults, they just wanted me to sing. Church became my place of peace, so any time things got crazy I went to church, and I sang my heart out which later helped my deliverance. Every time I would sing to the Lord, I felt this bubble in my stomach growing. I had a lot going on in my life at this point since my family was split; my mom left my dad again and my sister was now in the military. Mom was working hard to provide for me and my brother. Every dime I made went to buying clothes and nails or supporting my bad habit of cocaine. I really did not care about much else at that point. I learned to hide things from my mom well. I stayed in school and made sure my grades were excellent, so I did not have to hear my mom's mouth. I worked at a club here and there when I did not have a private party because as long as you looked older, they did not card you or care. I also had a part-time job at KFC which was my cover for late night parties.

This brings me to the next time I was raped in the bathroom of Magic City. I was so coked out of my mind I did not even tell anyone. For what? Nobody really cared anyways. I had become numb to so much. That was the last time I danced at the club and when I bought my first gun. I kept putting myself in danger and digging a deeper hole. I remember doing a private party one time and there was a shootout. Two men ran up in the house and just started shooting; two other girls and I had to jump out of a second-story window to escape. The next morning, I found out that four people died in that shootout and that one of them that had been killed was a dancer, but despite the news, that still did not stop me.

Chapter 3

By this time, I was dating two female dancers. I remember me getting sick and was unable to go out and make any money. They both brought me food and cash for a straight week. What did I need to dance for if they were going to fill my pockets and supply my drug habit? So, a few months before I turned seventeen, I put a plan in motion, and I started managing dancers. I was now balancing my family, school, a new boyfriend and two girlfriends; to this day I still do not know how I did it. I was bringing in good money and everything seemed to be going fine, until the day I had to use my gun.

I took my two girls to a bachelor party. I remember being in the back room counting money when an older gentleman came in. He decided he wanted me Instead of the strippers that were in the main room dancing. He dragged me by my hair, threw me on the bed and began trying to pull down his pants and holding my arms above my head with his free hand. I remember him smelling like cigarettes and cheap liquor. After he was finished with me, he got up to fix himself and walk towards the door; I scrambled to get back to where I left my gun. I set up and squeeze the trigger of my 9 mm two times. I watched as the man slipped to the floor. When the girls found me, I was still on the floor with no pants and underwear on. I had shot the man in the back of his shoulder blade once, and the other bullet missed and hit the wall. I had only practiced a few times in the woods. The blow back from the gun caught the skin between my thumb and my trigger finger. There was blood all over my hand. I dropped the gun from the pain. He was a lucky negro because for the first time I was mad as hell and I probably would have kept shooting. I promised myself no one would violate me again. I was wrong.

After that, my gun never left my side and I had no problem pulling it out and pulling the trigger; that was a traumatic experience that taught me a great lesson. Men did not respect women that were in this industry. They saw me as just another one of the girls stripping and having sex for money. I started to think that respect should be taken and not earned. I remember when I was younger, and my mama would say " stop crying - it happened! What you going to do about it now? Crying over spilt milk ain't never going to do nothing. You still have to end up cleaning it up." After those words it took a lot for me to cry. Why do we choose wrong when we know the right way to go? Even as a teenager I knew the life I was living was wrong; I just honestly did not care because I felt like no one cared about me. With all the family and the friends I had, I still felt like no one cared about or understood me. As much dirt I was doing and all the sneaking around and lying to my family, I truly believe low-key I wanted to get caught because maybe then they would see me and for once! I figured that they would see the depression, the anger, the hurt, the abuse and addiction and finally decide to step up and help me fix it.

Chapter 4

It was the summer before my last year of high school and I found out I was pregnant. Finally, I had someone that I knew would be all mine; someone I knew would love me no matter of the mistakes I had made or no matter how many times I made them. This also crushed the idea of me going to an out-of-state college. My mother was not happy about this. The "baby daddy" was cool of course and sold the family dream to me. I was young and did not even know what real love was, but I wanted that dream. I slowed everything down during my pregnancy - no more parties, no more girls hanging around, no more alcohol and a minimum use of cocaine. I gave birth to a beautiful baby boy on my eighteenth birthday and two months later I walked the stage and receive my High School diploma. This was the period of time that I felt the closest to my mom; she was certainly my support system. My boyfriend, AKA baby daddy, was now missing in action and that was after I found out his other baby mama had just given birth to their daughter a month-and-a-half before I had our son. Now the family dream was crushed but I did not care; I had a beautiful baby boy that was going to love me forever and I was going   to take care of him by any means necessary.

I had to pull it together because now I had a baby that depended on me. I could not just sit there and do nothing. I could not keep expecting mom to take care of us, so I dug in deeper. A friend of mine worked for a telemarketing company. She brought me home all kinds of credit card numbers and checks. My money was flowing once again, and I got my first apartment. I also caught my very first felony charge at the age of eighteen. I learned a few valuable lessons from my mistakes. The most important one was never to get caught again. I got caught up in a check scam and the police had no idea I was the ringleader even after they questioned me for hours. When I got arrested, I was so scared of going to jail that I would have told on my own mama even though she had nothing to do with anything that had taken place. My first charges were forgery and uttering. Even though that was the first and last time I got caught in that hustle, it certainly was not my last time doing it. Sometimes we take God's grace and mercy for granted. Trust and believe, you will know when God has decided to cut you off. 1st Samuel 16:1 says this:

" now the Lord said to Samuel you have more than long enough for Saul. I have rejected him as king of Israel."

There will be a time when God will reject you if you continue to play with His grace and His mercy. By the grace of God, I got out of that incident without much of a scratch, but that was the beginning of my now tarnished criminal record. The reason I could never have the career I wanted later in life. Still out on my own, I got into more trouble than ever; I also got pregnant again at the age of twenty. I was now a proud mother of two all while still being involved in two lesbian relationships with different women now and having sex with a man whenever I had an urge to do so. I did not necessarily hate men. In my mind, I wanted them to know that I had just as much power as they did and that no man would ever overpower me again; that was the lie that I told myself.

By the time I was twenty-one, I was in full swing of the life I had created. I had a beautiful townhome at the beach where me and my best friend did parties every weekend and managed a total of ten girls and six of them belonged to me, which meant most of that money came to me as well. The money that flowed through that house was unbelievable. I loved every minute of it. Having money meant respect and power to me and I wanted it.

Chapter 5

I was not the type female pimp that had to beat their women for control. I realized early on that these women were just as broken as me and all they wanted was love and attention, to feel special and be treated like a queen. Most of these women came from broken homes, broken relationships, had been beating on, raped and/ or neglected in way. I made every one of them feel special. The more love and attention they received from me, the more money they gave me, so I put a lot of time and energy into them. I have shut down nail salons just so all my women could get their manicure and pedicures done. They did not even know that they were being spoiled with their own money. Every once in a while, I had to deal with jealousy. I have dealt with just about everything from fights, to my car windows being broken. I believe all women can be bipolar at times.

I ran a very tight and profitable organization. My childhood best friend was the only one I trusted so she helped keep things running smoothly. The guys I knew started calling me "young gangster" because I played no games when it came to my money or my girls and I knew exactly where I got it from. My mother's side of the family was full of gangsters, so naturally I inherited some of their ways. To dance at my home or even become one of my girls you had to be interviewed and if you did not do VIPs you could not be a part of my team. I rendered services to men that they loved. The women were the product and they came in all shapes, sizes and color. Everything and everyone had a price at my house; from the alcohol to all the girls – neither could ever be described as cheap!

At this time, I was a full-time college student. My major was Business Management and I minored in childhood development. I loved school and my teachers were great. I literally lived five minutes from campus. I was living a life that I thought was amazing - everything else was buried deep down. I was now nonchalant about everything and bitterness and anger had taken root. I still did not see that I was leading myself to a very destructive path.

My weekend started early Friday afternoon, since by 5 p.m. my children were already gone for the weekend. All the girls that did not live with me had to be at the house by 8 p.m. and the party started at 9 p.m. I had two security guards - one was about a 350-pound security with a nice piece of Steel that was always at his side and he handled the door. The second security guard was my father. Yes, that is what I said, my father was one of my wingmen! He made sure the girls upstairs were safe. I had

29

a bartender in the kitchen that covered all kinds of drinks. I did not have any police problems nor neighbor problems. My neighbor was a bachelor and I took care of the police once a week. I was making more money than I had ever seen in my life. More importantly, I was well respected in the streets by all that knew me as "Lovely" which was the name my best friend gave me when I first started in the game.

Sometimes, I would have what we called lockout parties for big name rappers and singers that came through for concerts. I had a friend that worked at the scope; that is where all the concerts and wrestling matches took place. He would put me on to the ones who like to party after concerts. I was paid a large sum of money so they could have the house for the night. I provided an open bar, food and of course the entertainment. It is safe to say that I know quite a few people in the industry. I lived like that for over two years. It felt good to be able to put money in my mother's hand. I had the urge to prove to myself and to my mother that I could make just as much money as anybody else, that I was not a complete screwup and that even though my sister was in the military and had a great husband she was not better than me. Even after two children, two baby daddies and despite the two felonies and seven misdemeanors I had at that time, I could still be somebody my mother would be proud to call daughter.

Chapter 6

Of course, there were a lot of things I had to omit concerning my life at the time. I also wanted to prove to myself and others that a man could not do anything for me but put money in my pocket. I was so messed up in the head at that time. Have you ever tried to convince yourself that you were happy? Well that was me! I was trying to convince myself that money could answer all my problems. I was surrounded by people, but I was still lonely and depressed. I could have had any man or woman I wanted but I was insecure. Money may have changed my outside, but it did not change how I felt on the inside. I was still that sad girl that wanted my mother and father's approval and even though I was broken God still wanted me. He still called me.

I remember the night that I knew something had to change. I went to a church service with a family member. I remember this woman coming up to me and asking if she could pray for me and my children. I was never the type to refuse prayer. The Prophet begin to pray and stopped in mid-sentence. She looked at me and said " God said come out now! He has need of you!" Now, many people have prophesied to me, but it was something about what she said and how she said it. I heard urgency in her voice. I ignored the feeling and kept on living life. Less than a month later, my home, where I hosted all my parties, was shot up and destroyed. This was also the first time I decided not to be there when a party was going on because I decided to go out that night. I came home to cops surrounding my house, bullet holes through my walls, furniture torn apart and money missing. My father went to jail for possession of a concealed weapon, and I had three girls in jail for prostitution. That was my last party. I did not tell my mom anything about this until years later. At that time, I still felt like a screw up her eyes even though I was about twenty-three years old.

It was certainly time for a change. I was tired, depressed and tired of living any kind of way. I was tired of pretending that I was happy. I could fake a smile better than anyone I knew and could easily transform into the life of any party. There had to be more for my life than what I was doing - not just more but better. I wanted my children to have better and to be proud to call me mom.
One thing I have learned is that you can change your location as much as you want but you will still be dealing with the same situation; eventually you will have to face the problem, which is you! The most important people to me were my children. I wanted to make sure I had a safe environment for them, so I slowed everything down. I

started dancing again, but I hated it. When you are used to boss money, it is hard to go back to being an employee. My boys were now three and five years old and already having all kinds of problems in school. Children do what they see not necessarily what they are told to do, and trust me, my boys saw a lot when they were little. I put them both in counseling where they were both diagnosed with ADHD and my youngest was later diagnosed with bipolar disorder. Finally, I decided that something had to give. I was miserable and I felt like an even bigger failure as a mom.

I was at my breaking point and of course no one noticed until one day I snapped. I caught the young lady I was dating at the time cheating on me. I kicked door open, and at the front door, began beating her face with a lamp. It took two people to pull me off of her because I would not stop hitting her, even after she stopped defending herself. The next morning, my mother and her friend found me stretched on my mother's living room floor. I had taken over thirty pills - this became my first suicide attempt. Everyone assumed it had everything to do with the breakup. I did not care about her cheating since I did constantly. I was tired and angry.

34

Chapter 7

I had so much going on in the inside of me I did not know my up from down. I had a lot of pain and self-worth issues that needed to be dealt with. I had gotten so used to hiding in plain sight that the real me was invisible. I was placed on suicide watch at the hospital and then at my mom's house; for a while she did not let me out of her sight. I was trying my hardest to find myself, even though my family was in the middle of a crisis. I was slowly getting myself back together mentally after the suicide attempt. I start waitressing at. IHOP and even found my own apartment for me and my boys. It was during this same time that my brother had gotten into a car accident and we did not know if he would make it. My whole family came together to pray and give my mom support; that was the first time I had ever seen them come together like that. Mom's house was packed with cousins, aunties and close friends. I also found out I was pregnant again. This time I was being blessed with twins and I knew I would be having them alone. I had given up on having a normal family. I was fine with that because it gave me another chance of being a good mother. This was also the time my spiritual mother came into my life; God certainly sent her at the right time.

Our family was going through so much emotionally. The doctors had given up on my brother, but our family did not. I remember one particular Sunday; the whole family went to church to have the pastor pray for us. I had been to many churches and met many pastors, but it was something about this woman of God. (It helped that she was my sister's cousin on her father's side.) This was the beginning of a beautiful change.   I continued to go to church even after my brother made it through his crisis - only God could have performed this miracle since I know he was literally on his death bed, but God made death behave. Glory to God!!

I was happy for the first time in a long time, but that happiness ended very quickly. While my mother and my sister were in Oklahoma checking on my brother, I laid in a hospital bed alone, miscarrying both of my children at three months. Sadness and depression swallowed me again. I was told I could no longer have children. It was only by the grace of God that I did not lose my mind, but I now believe that everything I had experienced was bigger than me. The small faith I had begun to grow. Now, I was not perfect, and I still had a long way to go, but I said "Yes" to God and my process began. I was still smoking weed, but God gave me the strength to stop snorting cocaine and drinking - no Alcoholics Anonymous and no meetings. God literally took the taste from my mouth and I just quit. After almost eight years of using I just stopped. I no longer had the desire or urge to use again.

I got better; I started working again and got my own place in Norfolk. I was still partying a little and drinking when my husband came into my life. I still liked women and ran through them like it was nothing at all. He was a good friend before we ever started dating; I could tell him anything and everything. He knew my fears and my truth. He loved my children as if they were his own and was sweet, kind and gentle. God sent me a man that knew my past but still wanted to be a part of my future. We married in our second month of dating and I bore him a beautiful baby girl before our second year of marriage. She was our miracle baby. It did not matter what the doctor said because God gave us just what we wanted. My husband had no biological children and wanted to give that joy to him.

Chapter 8

God completely change my life around. Not only did he clean me up on the inside, but He brought me someone that understood my brokenness and had no problem trying to heal wounds he never created. He placed me in a ministry that did not judge me but loved me. God taught me how to love myself and to keep my head held high, even after I made a mistake. I realized that my past did not dictate my future. No matter what had happened to me or what anybody felt concerning me, I was a king's kid and no one could take that away, so my journey began, not in ministry but a journey towards a new and healthy life. My life truly began when I accepted salvation. My eyes were open to the things of God; it was almost as if God sat me in front of a mirror and began to compliment me. He told me how much he loved me and what I meant to Him. Then He began to show me who I could be and the purpose He had for my life. What do you do when someone saves your life? You devote yourself to them and that is exactly what I did. I devoted everything to God my Savior.

I became more involved in ministry. The closer I was drawn to God the more things fell off of me. I was changing and I loved it. I had I an incredible husband, three great kids and yet I was still angry. My Husband and I would get in terrible fights and I would destroy things in our house. I was so used to being in charge of everything; I did not really know how to submit to my husband. You cannot just put a pretty bandage on an infected wound and think it will heal on its own. I remember one fight we had when our daughter was just a few months old. He left and he did not come back for almost two months. I learned how to not allow things to go too far. He supported every idea and plan I had and did not even notice at the time that he did not get it in return.

Things at home were not great but I sure made it look good to everyone else as I grew in ministry. We eventually moved to North Carolina to start over. I had family there and it was very inexpensive to live. That is when I heard the call to serve as Pastor and once again, as he had many times before, my husband supported me. My mother shut down here businesses and moved to North Carolina as well and we started a church in our house. My ministry moved and grew quickly, and I loved it. I have had services where my entire living room was packed out and there was no place to even stand. I finally found my purpose in life - to help people that was like me and to lead them to Christ so they could experience his love and peace the way I did.

Everything moved so fast. I now had a large church that seated two hundred plus. My congregation was roughly fifty but everyone in town knew me and came to my services. I was preaching all over the state and God used me to do miraculous things. Prophesies would happen quickly. I would lay hands and heal. I was spending less time at home and did not notice at the time it was becoming a problem. Once again, I was in charge, the boss - different lifestyle same scenario. I learned quickly this was not what ministry was all about.

Chapter 9

I was at the top of my game in ministry when I found out I had stage four ovarian cancer. The church began to have problems and I had a split in my ministry because I trusted too easily. I went through chemo and radiation and continued to push through in ministry. I lost my hair and went through a few surgeries but kept fighting for the ministry and God's people. Despite my process I was a chosen vessel of God and this decision came before I ever came forth in the earth. Jeremiah 1:5 says:

"Before I formed you in the womb I knew you [and approved of you as My chosen instrument], And before you were born I consecrated you [to Myself as My own]; I have appointed you as a prophet to the nations."

This call became even more real to me as I was later anointed as an Apostle in His church. I loved doing the will of God and helping His people. It was still so much I did not understand in ministry, but I was certainly learning the hard way. I fought and beat cancer three times and never stopped the work of ministry. I had some setbacks, but this next situation almost took me out. I found out my husband was having an affair with the secretary of my church. She was also a good friend that I had moved to North Carolina.

I was devastated and almost lost my mind; I could not get it together. At this time, I was dealing with a son in a detention center and receiving treatment for now cancer in my small intestine. I was weak and tired. I remember one of my spiritual children that was very close to me saying "I've seen you beat so much in life. How can you fail behind a man," but he was not just a man, he was my husband and safe haven. If no one believed in me I knew he did. He was the glue that held me together. He was there through every church hurt, sickness and child problem.

This was the first time I doubted God; I just did not understand how this could happen. I felt like I was dying on the inside. I could not sleep or eat. A week later at around six in the morning I drove back to Virginia. Did I still have a church and members? Yes! Was I still called by God? Yes! I believe in leading while bleeding but not while I dying. The only thing that kept me from ending my life was my three children which had now grown up so much and understood everything that was happening. I moved in with my sister but immediately backslid to drugs and drinking to ease the pain for a short while. I also finished my chemo and had to start seeing a therapist. I still had to take care of my almost grown boys and my little girl, so I got a job as a waitress. Within three months, I had my own house. Before I knew it, my husband reached out saying that he wanted his family moved back home to be with us.

Things got better until I received a call that my father was in the hospital and needed surgery. My mother and sister and I quickly drove to North Carolina. When I saw my father, he did not even look like himself. The plan was after his surgery I would bring him home to live with me and my family. Despite my father's past, he was one of my biggest supporters in ministry. He was my head deacon and rarely missed anything. He was also the only real father my husband ever really knew.

After his surgery, my father never woke up; he could no longer breath on his own. I remember when we went to visit him and his sisters were there, my mom and sister. We prayed heaven down up in his hospital room. That is when I heard God tell me my father was about to die and I needed to prepare. I told no one but my sister. After almost a month in the hospital my father was gone. I could not even process anything yet. It was too much that had to be done. My father had no life insurance and no money, so we raise the money and had my father cremated. My sister was at my side the whole time. I was so thankful because I was still going through a lot in my marriage and ministry.

We had my father's memorial service in NC. I did not grieve until after me and my family got back home to Virginia. I felt like I could not breathe, but I still trusted God and his plan for my life. Not even two months after my father's homegoing service, my husband starting cheating again. He eventually moved out and moved in with one of the girls he was having an affair with. I allowed him to come back and forth for a while but grew tired of sharing my husband. He was now an angry man who blamed every problem we had on me, ministry and certainly God. He did not want me to preach or step foot in a church. The devil was a liar! That was not happening - ever! God had kept me all my life. I could never deny Him! I still did not understand why I was dealing with this. My assignment was still incomplete in North Carolina, so the Lord shifted me and my children back easily but alone. I prayed, cried, fasted and read my Word. I was trying my best to do what the Lord asked of me. Why would he allow this to happen again? Why would my husband keep hurting his family? I was hurt but most of all angry. At this point this man has been in my life for over ten years. I did not ask for any of this.

Chapter 10

It was not until God began to show me, me that I truly understood that it was not all of my husband's fault. Of course, he had no business cheating, that was his fault. So, what part did I have in this? Plain and simple, I put the church before my family. God gave me scripture after scripture concerning my failures as a wife and mother, not to hurt me but for me to understand but now it was too late. I could not trust him, and he had now turn into a man I did not recognize. The man that loved and supported his family was gone. He moved from one drug to the next and lied constantly. Eventually we talked and I was able to listen to him without cursing him out or hitting him with whatever was close by. The women he fell in love with were not preachers; he loved the loudmouth, bisexual go getter who would get high as a kite with him. This was a change he was not ready for or wanted for that matter.   I was no longer the same women he married. The change that saved my life was not a change he wanted nor was he willing to accept it anymore.

Everything in life can teach you if you pay attention to what is right in front of you. My lessons were not just for me but for the people I am assigned to serve. I have dealt with sickness, children behavior issues, marital problem, church hurt, family hurt and back sliding as a leader; you name it, I feel like I have done and dealt with it. I may have been wounded, but I did not die in it. What should have killed me eventually pushed me, but before that could happen, I had to be healed. Healing is a process and so is forgiveness. Until I was healed and learned how to forgive myself of past mistakes it was exceedingly difficult to forgive anyone else. Now I can look in the mirror and know that I am a great mom, a great person, a great leader and know I deserve real love. in spite of my past or my flaws I deserve to be happy. I do not mind starting over because He has made me new. I serve the God of a second chance. My story is not over because at the end I win!

2 Corinthians 5:17

Therefore, if any man be in Christ, he is a new creature: old things are passed away; behold, all things are become new.

CONNECT WITH THE AUTHOR

Author Reveena Blair

Email: newbeginning1505@gmail.com

Address:

60 Barber Street

Winston-Salem, North Carolina 27217

www.ingramcontent.com/pod-product-compliance
Lightning Source LLC
Chambersburg PA
CBHW070034110426

42741CB00035B/2761